GETTING TO KNOW
THE U.S. PRESIDENTS

MARTIN
VAN BUREN

EIGHTH PRESIDENT
1837 – 1841

WRITTEN AND ILLUSTRATED BY MIKE VENEZIA

CHILDREN'S PRESS®
A DIVISION OF SCHOLASTIC INC.
NEW YORK   TORONTO   LONDON   AUCKLAND   SYDNEY
MEXICO CITY   NEW DELHI   HONG KONG
DANBURY, CONNECTICUT

Reading Consultant: Nanci R. Vargus, Ed.D., Assistant Professor, School of Education, University of Indianapolis

Historical Consultant: Marc J. Selverstone, Ph.D., Assistant Professor, Miller Center of Public Affairs, University of Virginia

Photographs © 2005: Art Resource, NY: 3, 4 top right, 15 left (National Portrait Gallery, Smithsonian Institution), 4 bottom right (Reunion des Musees Nationaux); Bridgeman Art Library International Ltd., London/New York/New -York Historical Society, New York, USA: 4 bottom left, 22; Brown Brothers: 26; Columbia County Historical Society, Kinderhook, New York: 20; Corbis Images: 5 bottom (Bettmann), 4 top left, 17 (Francis G. Mayer); Hulton|Archive/Getty Images: 5 center, 19; Library of Congress: 18 right, 32 (via SODA), 6, 18 left; North Wind Picture Archives: 10; Spencer Collection, The New York Public Library/Astor, Lenox and Tilden Foundations: 11; Stock Montage, Inc.: 15 right; Superstock, Inc.: 5 top, 16; Texas State Library, Archives & Information Services Division/Eric Beggs: 30, 31; The Hermitage: Home of President Andrew Jackson, Nashville, TN: 25.

Colorist for illustrations: Dave Ludwig

Library of Congress Cataloging-in-Publication Data

Venezia, Mike.
  Martin Van Buren / written and illustrated by Mike Venezia.
      p. cm. — (Getting to know U.S. presidents)
  Includes bibliographical references and index.
  ISBN 0-516-22613-4 (lib. bdg.)   0-516-27482-1 (pbk.)
  1. Van Buren, Martin, 1782-1862—Juvenile literature. 2. Presidents—United
States—Biography—Juvenile literature. I. Title.
  E387.V46 2004
  973.5'7'092—dc22

2004000319

A portrait of Martin Van Buren as president by John Langendoerffer (National Portrait Gallery, Smithsonian Institution, Washington, D.C.)

Martin Van Buren was the eighth president of the United States. He was born in Kinderhook, New York, in 1782. Martin was the first president to be born a citizen of the new United States of America.

George
Washington

John Adams

All the previous presidents had been born during the time when the first thirteen states were colonies ruled by Great Britain and the King of England. George Washington, John Adams, Thomas Jefferson, James Madison,

Thomas Jefferson

James Madison

James Monroe

James Monroe, John Quincy Adams, and Andrew Jackson were all born as English citizens. They didn't become United States citizens until the Revolutionary War was over and the United States officially became an independent nation.

John Quincy Adams

Andrew Jackson

Martin Van Buren's birthplace in Kinderhook, New York

THE BIRTH-PLACE OF MARTIN VAN BUREN.

Martin Van Buren's parents owned a small farm in Kinderhook. For extra money, they made part of their house into a tavern. Travelers could stop for meals and spend the night there. Martin had lots of brothers and sisters. They were all expected to work on the farm and in the tavern.

Kinderhook was a beautiful town snuggled in the woods next to the Hudson River. Some people said Kinderhook was haunted! Martin and his brothers and sisters heard lots of ghost stories while they were growing up. Years later, the people of Kinderhook inspired author Washington Irving when he wrote his famous spooky story "The Legend of Sleepy Hollow."

The Van Burens' tavern was an exciting place. Many important leaders of the new United States government stopped there on their way to and from New York City and Albany. Albany was the capital of New York State.

Martin learned a lot by listening to discussions and arguments among visiting politicians and lawyers. He also loved the fancy clothes these wealthy visitors wore. He dreamed of having his own magnificent wardrobe someday.

The discussions Martin most enjoyed listening to in the tavern were about politics in the United States. Politics is the business of how a government is run. Politicians are people who are elected to government offices to represent everyday citizens. They are interested in using their ideas to guide and

Visitors having a conversation at a colonial tavern in the 1700s

The Hudson River south of Kinderhook in the early 1800s

shape the government of a city, state, or whole country. Mayors, state representatives, governors, senators, and U.S. presidents are politicians.

When Martin was fourteen years old, his parents arranged for him to be an apprentice to Francis Sylvester, a lawyer in Kinderhook. It was in Sylvester's office that Martin began to learn about the ins and outs of politics.

Martin worked hard in the law office. He cleaned floors, kept fireplace logs lit, and refilled ink jars. Since there were no copy machines at that time, he copied tons of law documents by hand. Martin read all kinds of books and articles about law, too. He learned about the ideas and goals different politicians had.

Martin especially liked the ideas of Thomas Jefferson, a man who would one day become president. Jefferson became Martin's idol.

Unfortunately, Martin's boss, Mr. Sylvester, didn't care for Thomas Jefferson's ideas at all. He tried to convince Martin that the ideas of another important American, Alexander Hamilton, were much better.

Alexander Hamilton believed the United States government should have a lot of control over the individual states. He also wanted the nation to have strong businesses and banks so that the United States would be able to stand on its own and not have to depend on other countries. The people who agreed with Hamilton formed a political group called the Federalist Party.

Martin Van Buren's boss agreed with the ideas of Alexander Hamilton (left),
but Martin preferred the ideas of Thomas Jefferson (right).

Thomas Jefferson believed almost the opposite. He didn't trust a strong central government and thought that average everyday people should have the power to govern their own states, counties, and towns. Jefferson organized a group, too. It was called the Democratic-Republican Party.

This painting by George Caleb Bingham shows Americans lining up to vote during an election in the early 1800s.

Even though Martin Van Buren disagreed with his boss, he was able to get along with Francis Sylvester. Martin always had a talent for being friendly to people, even if he didn't agree with them. Because Martin was so interested in politics, he decided to start helping people get elected to government jobs.

Martin worked hard convincing voters that his candidate was the best person for the job. During one election, Martin did such a good job of getting a candidate elected that the candidate rewarded him for it. He got Martin a better job in a big law office in New York City.

This is how New York City looked when Martin Van Buren got his first job there.

Martin (left) married Hannah Hoes (right) in 1807.

Martin Van Buren finished up his studies
in New York City when he was twenty-one
years old. He then returned to Kinderhook and
set up his own law business. He also married
his childhood sweetheart from Kinderhook.
Her name was Hannah Hoes.

An early steamboat on the Hudson River in New York

During this time, Kinderhook was growing from a quiet, sleepy village into a busy industrial town. The steamboat had just been invented. Now it was a lot easier for people, supplies, and products to travel up and down the Hudson River. Factories and businesses started popping up all over Kinderhook.

Martin soon had lots of clients. He became a well-respected lawyer and continued to help politicians he liked. When Martin was twenty-nine years old, he decided to run for a government job himself. In 1812, he ran for New York's state senate—and won.

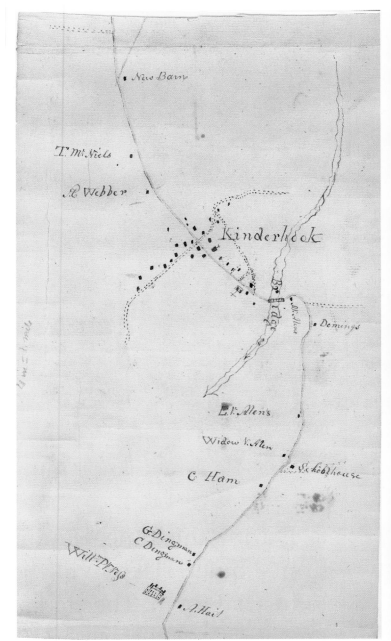

Kinderhook lay along the major road that led from Albany to New York City.

This was the beginning of an amazing political career. Martin ended up being elected to eight different political offices before he became president. He was a good politician because he knew how to please his friends while keeping his political enemies happy at the same time.

Martin Van Buren was a major force behind the project to build the Erie Canal. When people helped him get his favorite candidates elected to public offices, Van Buren rewarded them by giving them jobs on the Erie Canal project.

Early on, Martin Van Buren had learned the importance of rewarding people who helped him and his political party. When the Erie Canal was being built in upper New York

State, Martin made sure to reward workers who voted for him and his friends. He gave them jobs constructing the 360-mile-long canal.

Everything was going well for Martin until a tragedy happened. In 1819, Martin's wife died. Martin kept his mind off his sadness by raising his four sons and working harder than ever building his political power.

When Andrew Jackson ran for president in 1828, Martin Van Buren did everything he could to help him get votes. After he was elected, President Jackson rewarded Martin by appointing him to important government positions. When Jackson ran for a second term, he chose Martin Van Buren as his vice president.

Andrew Jackson was one of the most popular presidents ever. When it was time for him to step down as president, he recommended Martin Van Buren for the job. Jackson's support helped Van Buren win the presidential election of 1836.

A portrait of President Andrew Jackson by Ralph Earl

Standing Army, 200,000.

Laborers wanted to build poor-houses prisons &c NB Highest wages offered 12½ct's. per day

Sheriff sale several farms with cattle and farming utensils Second hand mechanics tools &c

SUB TREASURY OFFICE

PRISON

MECHANICS SHOP To Let

VAN BUREN AND RUIN.

In this historical cartoon about the Depression of 1837, a fat banker stands in the doorway as ordinary people weep because they have lost all their money.

Even though Andrew Jackson had been a popular president, he left a real mess for Martin Van Buren to try to fix. President Jackson had made some bad decisions when it came to running the money system in the United States. His decisions helped cause the country to go into a terrible depression.

A depression is a time when businesses do badly and many people become poor, often losing their jobs, savings, and even their homes. The Depression of 1837 wasn't all Andrew Jackson's fault. In the 1830s, banks had begun lending out more money than they really had to lend. Many people bought land and businesses with their loans. When more money was needed to keep the businesses going, the banks had nothing left to lend. Banks closed, and factories, stores, and farms went out of business.

Martin Van Buren didn't really know how to get the United States out of a depression. He did come up with a plan to set up a U.S. Treasury to control and protect money better, but Congress didn't approve it until 1840. By that time, the depression was pretty much over.

To make matters worse, as soon as Martin could afford to, he began dressing in the fanciest clothes money could buy. He also began to decorate the White House with

expensive furniture, carpets, and drapery. People who were losing their jobs and homes weren't too thrilled with President Van Buren's behavior.

President Van Buren also made some political decisions that some people weren't too happy about. When Texas won its independence from Mexico in 1836, Texans asked to join the United States.

A painting showing Texans fighting for their independence from Mexico in the 1836 Battle of San Jacinto

President Van Buren turned them down, though, because Texas wanted to be a slave state.

Slavery was one of the biggest issues in the United States at the time. Many people were for it, but lots of people were against it. President Van Buren wanted to avoid all the arguments he knew would start up if Texas became a state that accepted slavery.

Some Americans thought the president was weak and uncertain. Also, many people were upset with him for not doing enough to get the country out of its depression.

In 1840, Martin Van Buren lost the presidential election to popular war hero William Henry Harrison.

Martin Van Buren seemed to do a better job forming political groups than being president. By organizing large groups of people who worked together, Martin found a successful way to beat his opponents in elections. His ideas led to the way modern politics are run today.

Van Buren spent the rest of his life supporting his favorite candidates and writing articles that were against slavery. He died in Kinderhook, New York, in 1862, at the age of seventy-nine.